WITHDRAWN

YOU CAN DRAW
DINOSAURS

by Mattia Cerato

PICTURE WINDOW BOOKS
a capstone imprint

MATERIALS

Before you start your amazing drawings, there are a few things you'll need.

pencil

colored
pencils

paper

markers

eraser

ruler

SHAPES

Drawing can be easy! If you can draw these simple letters, numbers, and shapes, YOU CAN DRAW anything in this book.

letters

numbers

DSLU
VZ

1 2 3

shapes

lines

I C ◎

Y #

Fearless Boxer

Use Your Head!

Skater Dino

Batter Up!

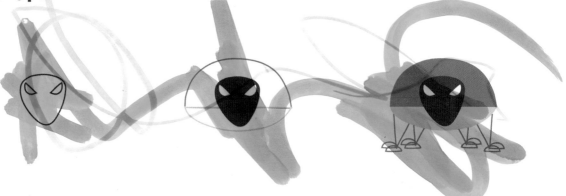

4

Now try this!

5

Winged Rocker

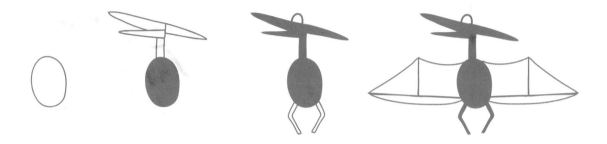

Feathered Drummer

Long-Necked Singer

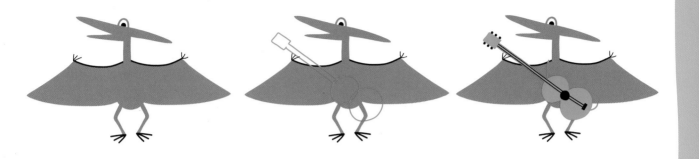

Dino Shopper

Snoozing Spike

Flipper

Plated Dino

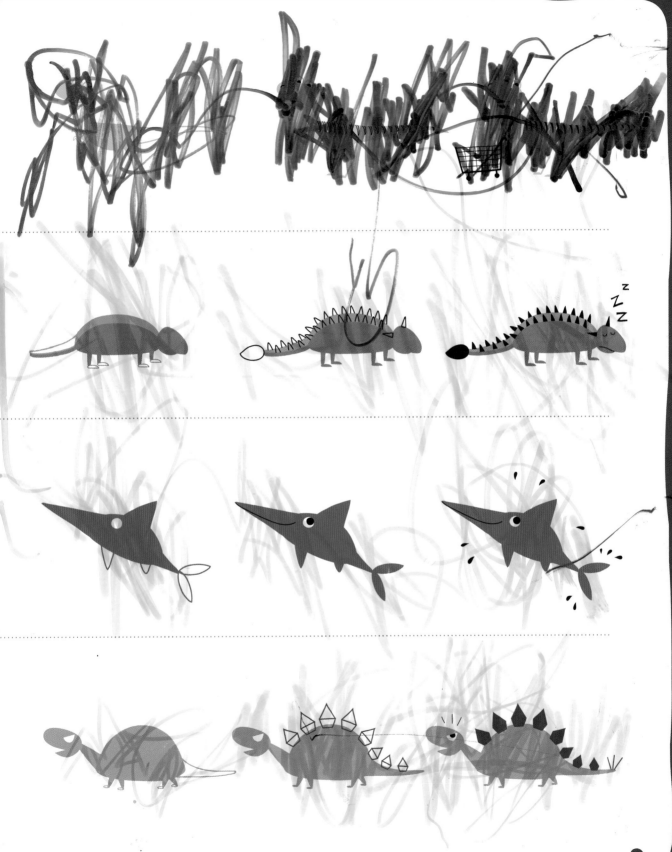

Out on the Town

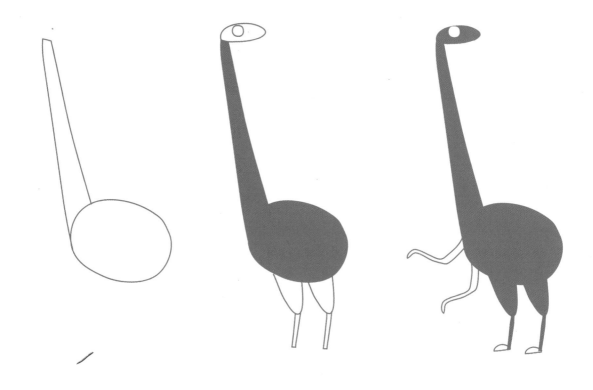

Armored Dino

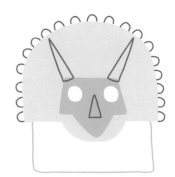

Time to Hatch!

Weight Lifter

Suspicious Spikes

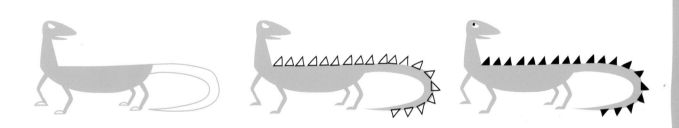

Dancing Dino

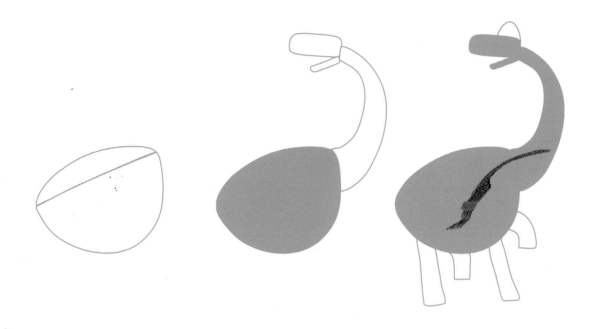

Dribbling Dino

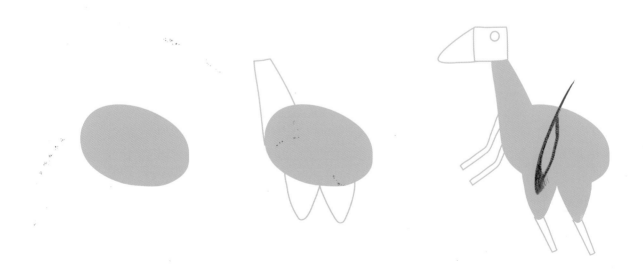

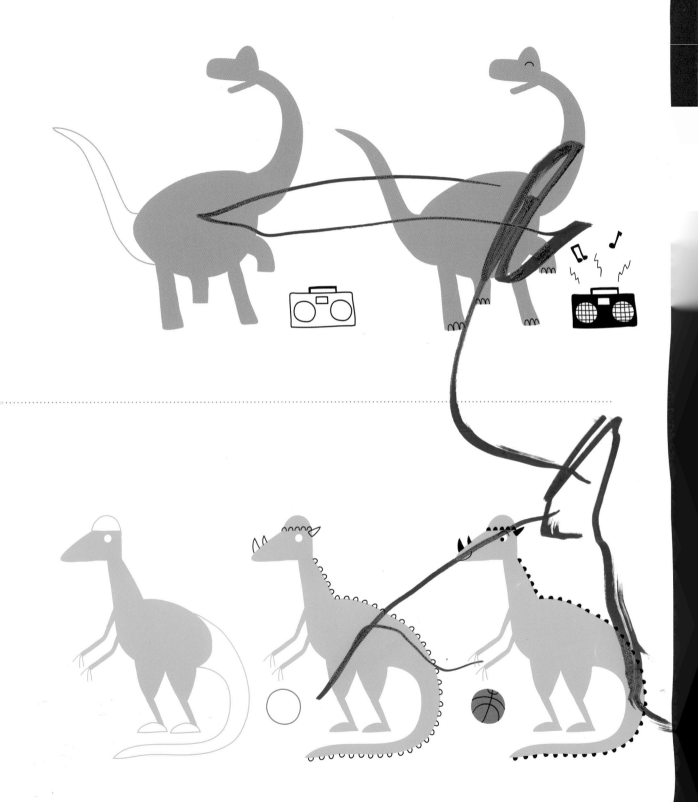

Watch Out!

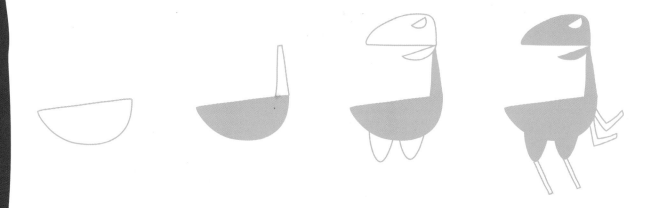

Small But Strong

Dino Racer

Waving Dino

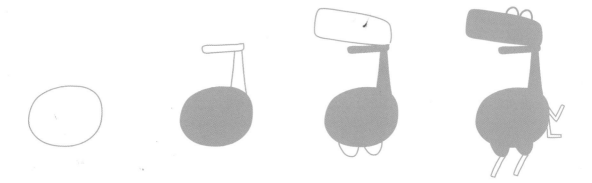

Egg Thief

Woolly Bully

ERUPTING VOLCANO

  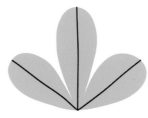 

PALM TREE

FERN

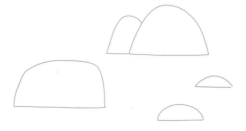  

ROCKS

HOT DOG

HOT DOG IN A BUN

STEAK

MUSTARD AND KETCHUP

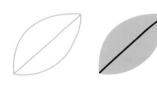

VEGGIE LEAF MEAL

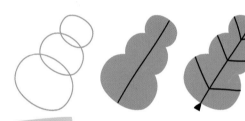

GRILLING

FORK AND KNIFE

TENT

All books published by Picture Window Books are manufactured with paper containing at least 10 percent post-consumer waste.

Library of Congress Cataloging-in-Publication Data
Cerato, Mattia.
  You can draw dinosaurs / by Mattia Cerato ; illustrated by Mattia Cerato.
    p. cm. — (You can draw)
  ISBN 978-1-4048-6280-7 (library binding)
  1. Dinosaurs in art—Juvenile literature. 2. Drawing—Technique—Juvenile literature. I. Cerato, Mattia. II. Title.
  NC780.5.B78 2011
  743.6—dc22   2010030023

Printed in the United States of America in North Mankato, Minnesota.
092010
005933CGS11

Picture Window Books
151 Good Counsel Drive
P.O. Box 669
Mankato, MN 56002-0669
877-845-8392
www.capstonepub.com

Editor: Shelly Lyons
Designer: Matt Bruning
Art Director: Nathan Gassman
Production Specialist: Michelle Biedscheid
The illustrations in this book were created digitally.

Internet Sites •

FactHound offers a safe, fun way to find Internet sites related to this book. All of the sites on FactHound have been researched by our staff.

Here's all you do:

Visit *www.facthound.com*

Type in this code: 9781404862807

Check out projects, games and lots more at
www.capstonekids.com

Look for all the books in the **You Can Draw** series: